ON BENDED KNEE (OBK): I'M A WIFE, NOT KNIFE

AUTHOR COLLABORATION FROM THE FAM 4 U SUB-MINISTRY: ON BENDED KNEE PRAYING WIVES GROUP

INTRODUCTION BY APOSTLE DANA NEAL

ISBN-10: 0988229358
ISBN-13: 978-0-9882293-5-8

For more information about Fam 4 U Breakthrough Ministries International, On Bended Knee Praying Wives Group, or Apostle Dana Neal call 414-301-1236

ACKNOWLEDGEMENTS:

I want to thank, the wives that joined me in creating this book. I want them to know that even after two years of trying, God knew I would delay, but he never denied US this opportunity. I thank you that you agreed to write a snippet of your life and help other wives around the world to see that no matter how good, or how bad things are, a marriage with God in it, is the best marriage of all; filled with favor, grace and mercy, you are WIVES and not KNIVES.

I salute you: **Tina Mull, Ailsa Hardy, Shelly Valasek, and Latisha Price**! I want to encourage you to step out and do all that God said to do. This book will catapult you into that next level.

Apostle D. Neal

INTRODUCTION

There are many times, a marriage goes through ups and downs. Even if the Lord brought two people together, there are challenges, trials, temptations, and tribulations, but in all that, if they endure, pray, fast till the end, they can make it.

God is the essential part of everyone's life. He is also the strand that holds marriage together if they let Him. The important part about knowing this is that, your marriage can't fail if God was (before the wedding) the head of your and still is; where do you see yourself right now?

OBK: I'm a Wife, Not a Knife was brought together to share testimonies and encourage others, but it's also for those of you that need direction, and help in where you are now. A knife cuts, and separates one thing into two; you don't want to be that person. A wife is a help meet, continuing to keep the bond of the marriage;

holding together the things that make you ONE.

Even if you WERE unequally yoked, you are still married and God honors that. Allow Him to release something from the pages of this book to your hearts and minds. God has something for every woman whether your marriage is perfect, just getting started, or has been going through turbulence. Don't give up!

Apostle D. Neal w/Fam 4 U
Breakthrough Ministries International

PRELUDE AND TRANSPARENCY:

When the thought came to mind to do this collaboration in 2012, I was not ready to 'partner' with anyone; God was pulling out of me what I didn't want to be pulled out. In turn, I was being disobedient in getting this project started and, then, completed. I was just Pastor Dana, trying to get my life right, my marriage right, and my ministry established; I was not ready to tell a story that was not necessary.

Now, it's necessary.

It is almost 2 years later that this book is being completed. We have less participants collaborating, but they are the most that have HIT HOME, and are helpful in this end result.

On Bended Kneed: I'm a Wife, Not a Knife is not your traditional book of testimonies; it is a self-help book from the hearts of real wives with real joys and challenges in their marriage.

This is encouragement for those that are getting married, are married or like me, separating.

Yes. Yes. It has happened to me. I am currently in the middle of a divorce. This roller coaster has really caused me to look at what it's like to go back to the single life as a ministry leader. God honors marriage, but He won't tolerate abuse of any kind from any side. As a wife, I was a knife; I wanted my way only, and when I did TRY to compromise, I was giving up a lot of how GOD MADE ME for someone who might not really know God.

It's important to wait on God and I didn't; our marriage, or even just our friendship, could have been a lot better IF I had. I love my husband; That won't change, but I had to walk away in order for my husband to see God in his life, and for us to be friends again.

It's been a toll on the son we have together and the children he helped raise, but the understanding right now is that you REALLY HAVE TO HEAR GOD WHEN HE SAYS WALK AWAY SO THAT THE OTHER PERSON CAN BE BLESSED, or sometimes, chastised.

Why is this part here before all the challenges and joys? Trials and triumphs? You have to understand that everything is not peaches and cream, but as long as God is in it, and you LET HIM DO THE WORK IN YOU (or your husband) that needs to be done, than the outcome can be very different. This prelude/transparency leads you to the first step in this book of encouragement and self help, and that is #CatchThat.

Blessings,
Apostle D. Neal

#CATCHTHAT

You can never be more or do more, without God by your side. When you walked down the isle to say, 'I do', and you knew in your heart that God wasn't in that, and He didn't bring that man to you, you were OUT OF ORDER, and needed to SHUT IT DOWN.

No ma'am, it didn't matter how embarrassed you would have been or how much money you spent; obedience is better than sacrifice and you were not in obedient. #catchthat

I remember when I heard the Holy Spirit say to me that my husband was going to ask me to marry him; we weren't even living right, but I heard it. It was the year I moved in with him but three years before he actually proposed. God gave me time to #catchthat, but I didn't. The problem is I didn't listen to the rest of the message. When prophecy is given in parts you have to wait on the rest to know what to do; I found this out SOME MANY YEARS LATER.

With all that was mentioned in the prelude, I must say to you, that your #catchthat moment is now! You can't keep waking up in trials and say that we're (your marriage) is blessed just because of waking up; you have to ask God, and receive the answer, as to why HIS GRACE AND MERCY allowed you to wake up. What needs to change? What needs to be worked on? Do you need some type of REAL CHRISTIAN COUNSELING? Are you angry about past hurts, or just trying to love on someone that visibly doesn't love you?

Or better yet, your marriage is great, God blesses you both, and you are the help meet to your king. What is God showing you that you need to do to help others? How can you help the single ladies get ready for their 'Boaz'? You're a Wife, Not a Knife in any part of your marriage and this teaching others, too. #catchthat

HE'S ENOUGH
BY ROCHELLE VALASEK

Every time we share with someone that we are married high school sweethearts we get the typical, "Oh, how sweet!" and the "Wow, you must have been together a long time! That's great!" To be very honest, it's not cute, and it's very hard work. Yes, all marriages are hard work, but when you fall in love as teenagers and get married right out of college, you are still growing into adults. What you had in common while dating and even in the beginning of your young marriage, it will change because God is still molding you into who you are to be. You will become two different people without you even knowing it.

It is said when your children leave the nest, that not only do you get the 'empty nest syndrome', but you look at your spouse and say, "Who are you?" You get so caught up in your children when they come into the picture that you don't see yourselves changing their either. As if being married and parenting is hard enough, those who marry young as high school sweet hearts have to deal with growing up at the same time as two individuals. I'm not speaking of the vows that say 'Let they two shall be as one'. I'm talking as individual children of God.

I believe as women it is even a harder situation to deal with. Women tend to be more emotional. We tend to be more attached to the little memories our mates tend to forget and look as minor things. For example, what you were wearing on the first date, or what song was playing during our first dance or first kiss. Most of them just don't keep those things in mine. I'm not bad mouthing them, that's just the way they're built. If you have one of the men who do remember those things…I congratulate you.

And indeed, that is one of my problems. Well, I learned, but I still have my moments. I'll be honest with you. I remember the first kiss. I know where it was, I know what it was like, and I know it was about 8 days after we dated. I can remember when he'd always grab my hand wherever we went. He couldn't keep his hands off of me. (I mean that in a polite way.) I recollect that he would always remember me when he would go shopping and buy me my favorite candy bar or soda pop. I loved and admired how he treated me like I was so smart and beautiful and that I was the only woman on the planet for him. There are so many ways he made me feel wonderful, alive, and loved.

But then, the kids are older, 15yrs and 18 yrs., on in college and one in high school. If that isn't hard enough, my 15 year old has special needs. I get to feel alone, not only emotionally, but in the battle. My husband got caught up in his work the last few years. (Sometimes I think it's to escape everything at home.) And when he comes home he goes straight for the television or games. As if no one is around him. I no longer get my hand held, I no longer get touched with a loving hand, the calls, the little surprises, the respect of being intelligent and such is gone. As all of this is happening, I'm starting to get frustrated, feeling disrespected, and confused. What happened? What did I do? Yes, there are many elements, and he's not all to blame.

I knew the fact that I had to work on myself. I can't change my husband, only God can. And that is only if my husband wants and lets Him. But the one thing that was missing was I still was feeling alone and unloved. Yes, I know many friends and family love me, but I'm talking the spousal kind of love. That best friend, confidant, unconditional love like no other, warm and fuzzy love and more. While I work on myself, where is that? I prayed and prayed for my husband to change QUICK! I was in need of the old him. I wanted the 16 year old I fell in love with. And then God began to speak to my heart. He reminded me.

1) I can't put time on God's work.

2) I can't wait to work on myself while waiting for that "hole" to be filled by my husband.
3) <u>GOD IS ENOUGH!</u>

God is enough! Wow! That hit me! One of those things you think you should know, but somehow it got lost in your mind and heart somewhere. It was like a whole new revelation again. God fills all my needs, even the needs of my husband. While God will always be there for me, at the same time, while I'm waiting on my husband, God is enough.

ROCHELLE VALASEK IS A WOMAN OF GOD, WIFE, MOM OF 2 BOYS LIVING IN NASHVILLE, TN. SHE IS ALSO A CHRISTIAN COUNSELOR, SPIRITUAL HEALTH COACH, SPEAKER, AND AUTHOR. SHE ALSO HAS BEEN HONORED WITH A DOCTORATES OF DIVINITY IN 2007. SHE HAS A DEVOTIONAL FOR MOMS

AND A BIBLE STUDY OF
THE PROVERBS WOMAN.
SHE IS PRESENTLY
WORKING ON HER
FOURTH BOOK. ROCHELLE
LOVES TO HELP ENLIGHTEN
WOMEN WITH BIBLICAL
TRUTH TO ACHIEVE
HEALING AND SPIRITUAL
HEALTH THROUGH GOD'S
UNCONDITIONAL LOVE.
YOU CAN FIND HER AT
WWW.ROCHELLEVALASEK.C
OM.

Apostle Dana Note: I hadn't realized God was enough, until I was at the crossroads of serving (both God and my husband). When the realization hit, I was ready to love my husband enough to leave him, and let GOD LEAD him.

BITTER SWEET BUT ALL GOOD
BY AILSA STOKES (HARDY)

Marriage has been a roller coaster ride for me, not only of ups and downs, but blows and woes. I played house with my now husband for about 15 years. We have three lovely sons ages 21, 18 and 10. As of this time we have been married for 7 years. These past 7 years has taken me up, and taken me down, and I imagine he has been through the same thing. That is one thing in marriage that we must remember that there really are two people. The word of God in Matthew 19:6 say *Wherefore they are no more twain, but one flesh. What therefore God hath joined together let no man put asunder.* I think about this a lot; trying not to add or take away from God's word.

We are no longer two, but we become one flesh. One flesh what is that? Do we look at it like God has taken two people and made them into one person? That's a question I am yet seeking the answer for. If I look at this word I see two become one; huuuum does that mean that we only have one mind now, one thought, one body? I have put out some questions and can't provide the answer but what I can offer here is this.

With God in the midst of your marriage it is all good. There are some things we try to break down and analyze but I really don't believe all that is necessary. Will we ever understand what God is saying here? If we say we trust Him at His word and we believe and we have faith then I don't think there is much that we need to do about going much deeper with trying to understand what God is letting us know here.

I don't think that we need to understand everything. When we push, and push our minds to understand every inch of everything that goes on, we welcome in confusion. But with God in the midst, wow, it's all good. Marriage will take you into some places that you really may not want to go. There has been so much going on in the past 3 years of my marriage I had to call this chapter: bitter sweet, but all good.

At the beginning of the nuptials things where good. We were ready to move on with our lives to live for Jesus! To do things right by Gods eye. We had been living in sin for so long we had to go this way and it was the right thing to do. Now the past three years of marriage for me and my husband is where the bitter begin to take its form. First let me share this poem with you then we will proceed:

Never Should Have Been Told

Rescued by what I thought was a genuine soul
But wasn't there was a story that just got told
Mixed up in a world of deceit
He pounded my heart with both feet

He looked me in my eyes and
confessed his past
A place of comfort I had to find real
fast
Me and at least a half a dozen others
Could have been his babies mothers
But God covered me
Because my eyes could not see
My life that God gave
His selfishness could have put me in
the grave
What was done in the dark has been
brought to light
Hurt, confused I'm still trying to hold
on with all my might
They say forgive and move on
But how all the trust is gone
20 years with what I thought was a
good man
Has been deplenished in a moment of
quick san
I said I do till death do us part
It has stop beating yes my heart
Rescued by what I thought was a
genuine soul
I wish his story have never been told

I wrote this poem in March of 2010;
that is when my husband had took me

to a place I knew with everything in me I would never have to visit. My husband had told me just two weeks prior to writing this that he had been with other women in the beginning of our relationship. That he had been cheating on me for the first 10 years. He had shared with me details, times, places, and people. That may seem to be a little hard to believe that a man would share such details; well I asked him to because I really didn't understand what he was saying. I needed to know I needed to understand, wow, allowing confusion in. I really could not fathom my man doing this. There was just no way.

That may seem a bit crazy because the old saying is that a man will be a man, or wait here is one better, all men are dogs. I thought I had been blessed with one of a kind. See, my now husband was always nice, polite, humble, he was a quiet man. I never let the thought of the old saying the quiet ones, are the ones you have to look out for. Wow! He never went out. He never did much of anything, but go to work and go to school that was it and that was all (oh so I thought). You could count on one hand how many times he went anywhere without me. Even to his family house. We did everything together. So I thought.

Bitter sweet, but good. About three years ago, or so, just before he felt compel to share his hidden secretes with me we had started going to church together as husband and wife. Even when I didn't go he was there. This was something so new because all the while we have been together we was in the world doing our thing. We both drank, and had fun out there together but I was going to church. He wasn't into church like that. He believed in God and all, but churching wasn't for him. Some time before this, his boss asked him to take over the theology class at the school he was teaching at; When he shared that with me a feeling hit me right in my belly. I told him you are being set up, and God will get the glory from this. I told him God was in the mist of this.

He was just like yeah ok, but not soon after we started going to church together. Then out the blue, bitter hit us in the face.

Well, the sweet had become bitter at this point. My husband really tore me up, not just in my heart but in my soul. I wanted to have some revenge because a couple of the ladies he had been seeing I had asked him about, but he assured me that I was crazy to think such a thing. I believed that, too. I had to be crazy because of the facade that he had played and I had believed. Even then there was something wonderful being worked out. God don't make mistakes man always do. One main reason we tend to make mistakes so much, is that we have a need to understand everything that happens in our lives. We just need to know that with God in the midst it's all good. Let me also share this. I wasn't a saint by any means, and can't make it out to look like my husband is just the bad guy here.

I could spend some more time going deeper about things that transpired from the secrets that my husband shared but the important part here is to let you all know that marriage will have its ups and downs, and its ins and outs. What you chose to do with them and how you chose to play them out will solely depended on you. The word gives us instruction on all that we need to know. It even tells us that there is nothing new under the sun. So whatever can happen in a marriage there is help in the word for it.

Some Christians don't speak much about divorce except about how God don't like it. I am not here to say what to do, but I know this, never make a choice without consulting God. God is the best advisor you have to call on. Marriage will surely have you calling up that number a many times. Bitter Sweet but all Good.

I chose to stay with my husband for all the wrong reasons, but God. God is a loving merciful God, and I think back to how He kept me and gave me chance after chance with all the wrong that I have done in my years. When my husband was out there doing his thing, God was watching over me protecting me covering me. I am so thankful for that. Whatever the situation was that he felt he needed to venture out, God was saying I love you my child I'm protecting you even as you sleep. And in marriage that is what we have to do protect our husbands even while they sleep.

If you are not yet married, you pray and ask God to send your husband; the one that He has designed especially for you. God will do it. Don't rush it. You may say you are lonely that you are sick of being alone. Well, I'll tell you this, your sweet don't have to be bitter when God has His hand on it. We are the ones that rush into things and become anxious just ready for the man to say I do. Well allow God to place the, I do in his mouth so that when he says it he will.

If you are already married, I know you can relate to some of the things I have said. Are we perfect? Are there some things we have done that wasn't pleasing to God? In His word, He lets us know that marriage is not for everyone that some folks are just too immature to handle the seriousness of marriage. The one thing people do quick fast and in a hurry, jump to the nasty D word: divorce and it really isn't that serious. When your husband or wife makes a mistake, in marriage we have to be strong enough to believe God at His word. All things work for the good of those that love Him. Ask yourself when your sweet becomes bitter do you love God enough to allow things to be worked out for your good?

So, let me say this even after the secrets have been let out of the darkness we are yet together, working it out with the Lord. We are yet rocky, but I trust that however it plays out we will receive the good because we love the God. In marriage there are going to be some times when one spouse wont to literally take something and connect with the other mean wanting to just go up side their head, but we can't do that. When you love the Lord we have to maintain our relationship with God more so when we get married because when we become one, we have allowed our husband or wife in our space. We will need all the divine help we can get. Let us remember that no one is perfect, some mistake will be made, and that your marriage will not only have bitter sweet moments but it will be all good.

Apostle D. Neal note: Bittersweet is a good lesson to have in any marriage.

LOCKED UP AND FREE
BY: TINA S. MULL

Submitting yourselves one to another in the fear of God. Wives submit yourselves unto your own husbands as unto the Lord. For the husband is the head of the wife, even as Christ is the head of the church: and he is the savior of the body. Therefore as the church is subject unto Christ, so let the wives be to their own husbands in everything. Husbands love your own wives, even as Christ loved the church, and gave himself for it... Ephesians: 5:21-21(KJV)

All my life I have desired to be married to a wonderful man who would provide for me and our children, to live in a big house with a white picket fence; maybe have about four children total, two boys and two girls and may a dog and a cat. This was me as a young girl who was naïve and unknowledgeable. It truly takes God and the Holy Spirit to turn a naïve, young girl into a woman who has gained wisdom and obtained knowledge. There is absolutely no other way.

I am now grown up; I have gained some wisdom but yet still acquiring knowledge. I have also gotten married to the love of my life who happens to also be my best friend. We have spent most of our married life in the unthinkable type of marriage and there were many times when I didn't think I had enough energy deep within me to endure. I didn't think that we would make it through but with the strength and power provided by the almighty God... we have been able to weather the storm for the past seven years.

Although when many look on the inside at our marriage, they see two people who seemed to be locked up, the truth is we are really in essence, *"free"*. We are free to Live, to Love, to Commit, to be Loyal to one another, to Triumph, to Serve God with our whole hearts, and to Celebrate this marriage that we were blessed to enter into together in covenant with God. No matter what it looked like (past tense), we have had the power to persevere.

This is our story through my eyes with tears of joy for being free. We are free today even though my husband has been behind bars and I am thankful to God that we are Free.

Over seven years ago in May of 2005 there was only thing that I was sure about was that if God had ordained my marriage, he would see me through the situation that we were about to face. When my husband proposed to me, he was in a lot of trouble. (*A little background*) Before we had gotten married we had been living together for almost 17 years, both living an unsaved life in the sin of the world. When I finally decided that I was tired of many things that were taking place in my life, I decided to give my life over to the Lord--- I remember that day if it were yesterday on June 30, 2004. Life had become different for me and the things that I used to do, at that time, had no more barring. I was still living in the same house as my children's father (now my husband). I had finally gone to him and let him know that I had decided to turn my life over to God which would drastically change things between him & me. No more sharing the same bed, no more living in sin also I clearly told him that any hopes of a sexual relationship was definitely out of the question. At first it wasn't an issue but the more that I changed, the more things began to get difficult for us. He began to question where I went, who I was with, how I acted, and who I had become. The devil had begun to rise up to the cause deep within him, the more that I said, "No" the more that he persisted especially in the area of sex. It was funny to me because we hadn't had a regular intimate relationship for many months. It had been sporadic because there were cases where we had gone without having sex when I wasn't saved. I knew the enemy was attacking me on a regular basis, so I told him that it was time to part ways and he had to move out. I first gave him a 30-day notice which turned into a 60-day notice then a 90-day notice. I truly loved him with all my being which caused me to pray to God for him to get saved, for my family to stay together, for us to get it right God's way. It seemed like the more that I prayed the harder things got. He fought me about church, about praying, about reading God's word, about paying my tithes, about giving an offering, about simply all that I done for God. It got to be so difficult to bear that I began to tell God if this is what I have to go through than I don't want any of it. I wanted him out of my house and out of my life for good or so I thought. My mind said this with every ounce of my being but my heart said something totally different. Shortly after, the Lord had begun dealing with me in dreams about my husband... I had one dream for four days straight and little did I know that this dream would truly change our life forever. I didn't believe that such a change could take place but it did. The Lord always delivers a warning before destruction. He showed me a vivid picture of my husband's future- he was about to have an encounter with the police that would do exactly what I had asked— remove him from my life. That Friday afternoon I waited patiently at work for him to pick me up and ironically he never showed up, it was because he had been arrested by the police for a major drug deal gone badly. I had heart pains so bad that I thought I would die. Our children were at home and he had been taken off to jail. Once I got home, I immediately called my Pastor because I knew that I wouldn't make it through the night. I had to do something, I had to do anything, and I couldn't lose him like that. I loved him too much. I didn't sleep for days on in. I was so sick that I had to take off work until I knew the answers to solve my current situation. Days turned into weeks, it had been nearly a month before I got a call from one of his attorneys who said to me go get him out now while his bail has dropped down to $1000. His bail was nearly $25,000 since he had been arrested. I took the last $1000 that we had, drove downtown and got his bail posted for his release. We had to hire a public defender to represent him; financially we couldn't do anything else. We weren't out of dark yet. We still had a long road ahead of us.

We had to move from our 3-bedroom townhouse into a very small 2-bedroom apartment to fight the case. We had begun to sell things in order to live. All of the money that he had was seized by the police and declared "drug money". We'd never see any of that again. During the course of the trial, I began to feel an enormous amount of hatred towards this man… how could he do this to 'us', to our children? I felt so humiliated. In my mind, he wasn't worth my time anymore--- Operation Good-bye--- I knew deep down from the pit of my emotions that we could never make it. I had decided all of this inside of my own mind. I had even tried to replace him with someone from my past but later on down the line I found out that wouldn't work because in the mist of all the court dates, my husband had found the one thing that could save his life as we knew it. He found a relationship with God. He had made up in his mind that he couldn't make it alone and needed something more powerful than himself to see this thing through. On January 2, 2005, he went to church with our children and the Lord was a new part of his life. On that day I could feel the Lord pulling at my heart deeply to go to church with my family but I hesitated. After service at my church was over as I drove, I ended up in front of the church. When I walked into the church I was amazed at what I saw, this man had his hands up with tears streaming down his face. I still didn't understand what was going on because I had changed my mind and I didn't want God to do anything that would come remotely close to us getting back together. I was still so hurt, angry, frustrated, betrayed, and didn't want my life to be where it was at that moment. I didn't feel like I deserved any of it. Why me? All I could hear is God saying why not you? At that present time when I walked into the atmosphere, the Pastor of the church called me down to the alter to be with him and our children. He openly admitted to me in front of our children, the Pastor and before God that he wanted our relationship to work out and he wanted us to be married. It brought such a nasty taste to my mouth because at that time, I didn't feel the same. Through all the famous court hearings, we found out that he was facing 43 years in prison. I cried so hard but I couldn't understand why. It was because deep down inside, no matter what I said out of my mouth, I wanted this man apart of my life more than I wanted to admit. But little did I know was that during the process that we were going through at that present time, we weren't alone. God was with us every step of the way orchestrating a few things. He was honoring my very first request which was for this man to be my husband as I had asked with my whole heart and for our lives to be joined together in destiny. It would only be a matter of time before I saw what he had really been doing in the mist of all that chaos going on around us.

One day, while I was at work, I received a phone call and it was him other the other end and he had decided that he wanted to set up a meeting with me, himself and my Pastor. He had quite a few things that he needed to get off his chest because he knew that he loved me so deeply and wanted us to become married, and I didn't act like I wanted the same. We needed help at that time because we both were saved claiming to serve God but didn't act as such. At that time, I knew we should go because I felt like my Pastor would be a good candidate to set him straight but little did I know that I would be set straight in that same visit. There were many things that I had been doing that were out of order as well. In my mind, I didn't think that I had been behaving badly because I felt like I was the victim; I knew that I was right and on the other hand he was completely wrong. When we had our first meeting, I listened to his outpour of feelings come out about love, how he wanted his family then marriage---

these were all things that I hadn't considered for quite some time. Why not? Because I had changed my mind... I didn't think that I wanted those options anymore mentally but deep down within my heart I had been hurt. All this new hurt had took me back to a place in our past where he hurt me so much and I allowed everything to consume me with anger, hatred, and un-forgiveness. That was not pleasing to God's eyesight and my husband knew that. He asked me if I would pray ask God for forgiveness, ask God to help me to forgive him and also ask him to help me to forgive myself for all the cruelness. He said then once you have done all that then if you still say no to us getting married then I will step aside and allow you to do whatever it is you plan to do. I agreed. After our conversation I went into prayer and consecration over the next four to five weeks asking God for His will for us, for a forgiving heart, for strength, for guidance and direction. The more that I prayed, the more the Lord began to reveal to me different things about myself, the fact that I was afraid of many different things, that I wasn't sure about what I wanted to do, and also that I had to forgive if I wanted to be forgiven. At that time I had to be willing to let go and let God. The reason why I was so unsure was because I knew he was about to leave for a substantial amount of time and we had never been apart that long. I was afraid for our children. More importantly I was afraid of His relationship with God. Would he be able to hold on to what God had done in his life and be the man who I needed him to be? It wasn't my business. Only God could make the necessary changes within him. Once all those things took place within me our real problems began to unfold. We went back to court days after I came out of prayer and he ended up with a guilty plea and that 43 years just became a reality. How would I do this? Marry a man whose life could possibly be spent in prison. At that time I knew the answer so clearly, I will trust God!!! We were still meeting with my Pastor at least once a week. I had secretly decided with God's guidance to accept his proposal, and in a couple of weeks it would be my 32nd birthday. A couple weeks before my birthday in our session, I revealed to him and my Pastor that I had accepted his proposal and for my birthday gift I wanted to go get our marriage license to get prepared for our wedding. Our counseling sessions then were marriage counseling. Together we set out date for May 21, 2005. We decided that we would do a small, intimate ceremony before God and a few important family members and close friends only. At that time I didn't know what I was doing but I trusted in God knew exactly what he was doing. Everyone around me thought I had gone crazy and so did I, but I knew that if I wanted to really step out on faith I was in a good place. *Now Faith is the substance of things hoped for and the evidence of things not seen. (Hebrews 11:1 KJV)* I had to trust Him at his word and if he said that this man was my husband then He wouldn't take him away from me for 43 years. He would have mercy on his life and for my husband's sake; I knew God was of His word. Now I had come to the place where I would stand on the word of God for my soon to be husband. On our wedding day, he was already found guilty so we continued to go to court for sentencing which was postponed twice. Once he had finally gotten sentenced, he had been home for four months with his family. He finally got his sentencing where he was sentenced to 20 months on a case where he was facing 43 years. It was a blessing because no matter what anyone said, I knew God did that!!! He had mercy on my husband's life that day. He went in September 2005 then returned May 2007. That time flew by for us. We were back together again and now would be our time to experience freedom that only God can provide…

New to all of this, it was a major struggle as being a wife, mother, who was unemployed when I was used to working a full-time job. I lost my job due to illness and major surgery. I didn't know exactly how to manage my time effectively. I had started back working towards my Associate Degree but that wasn't enough. I had lost my job back in 2006 while my husband was in prison, so when he came home I was receiving unemployment benefits roughly totaling $380 ($355 + $25.00 stimulus payment) and barely making the rent payments. So now that my husband has been released from prison to a wife who was financially stressed out but also later to find out he had no job as well. He was originally told that upon release from prison, he would be able to keep his job but then that fell through. So now we both face the situation of how do we keep a roof over our head, pay our bills, and also love one another when the times had gotten so stressful. There were days when we were barely able to speak without arguing. We weren't able to see God working in the mist of all our anger and frustration. We needed an outlet. Many things for us had begun to change. I knew that I had to do something so I began praying more that I wouldn't lose my husband to the streets and that he wouldn't lose his faith in God. I did this on a daily basis and I cried nightly. I never expected for things to be like this. It had gotten unbearable because now my husband had moved away from me far beyond my reach. There were things that he had wanted me to do that I had refused. I didn't want to move out of our house down to his family's house in the hood, I was afraid we would lose our sons to a life of drugs and murder. I didn't want to cancel the cell phones, or the cable or the internet... No No No!!! Why should we have to settle??? I literally pushed my husband over the edge by allowing us to live above our means because now my unemployment has ended and his hustle began- no job, no money, no food, big bills and things had to change—he put God down and picked up a sack. He was able to hide it from me for months. I didn't pick up on it right away; I literally had to stumble on things one day when I washed his clothes. I found the evidence in one of his pockets, the more that I looked, the more I found. During the entire time I was too busy to even listen to what the Lord had been trying to tell me about all the decisions I had tried to make on my own. Once again inside my mind, I hadn't done anything wrong; I didn't need to submit to him, he needed to submit to me. I was the one who had waited for him over the past 20 months holding things down. I never took the time to listen to my husband's cry for help. Our rent was over $800, cell bills running over $600 most months then we had cable, internet, electric and gas, food, household items, toiletries. We also lived the same way that we were used to living when we both had a substantial income but now we barely had anything. I can't begin to blame everything on myself nor could I blame everything on him. We both were utterly frustrated at the position we were in. The things that were had faced were things that we had never faced before and the truth was that we didn't know exactly how to handle it at that time. We had always been able to pay our bills when we was out living in the world and things always seemed so easy for us but now it was just the opposite. The other thing that was different now we were married and just couldn't walk out of the door. That would have been much too easy just to walk away. There was something that we both had to do especially if things were to turn out his way. "Obedience is better than sacrifice". (*1 Samuel 15:22 KJV*) God's way would be the only way. We both had to do it in order for things to work out in our life. It had become hard and the more that I began to badger my husband about his choices, the further I pushed him away, and the more frustrated that he became. The nights got longer and the days got colder. We were falling apart at a rapid pace. Communication had become a nonexistent part of our marriage. He didn't want to hear me speak to him about the things that had been going on. He refused to pray because he believed that his prayer wouldn't be heard or answered because if they would then we would not have crossed the road to get to the place that we were in at that time. I began to beg my husband not to give up but to Trust God because I knew deep down inside that the God I had come to know would not fail. He wouldn't leave us or forsake us. (*Deuteronomy 3:16 KJV*) I could think clearly back to the 43 years and how things had turned out for us the first time. I knew that he was a God of a second chances but it would be hard to get Mr. Mull to see exactly what I had seen. At that point he was filled with hopelessness and despair. I knew that I needed to speak life over my husband, and directly into him. When I felt like I had run out of options I decided to call our Pastor and schedule an appointment for him to meet with my husband. The next obstacle was getting him to go there and hopefully this would help out some way. I was so thankful that he agreed to go to the appointment but guess what???? He didn't open up, he refused to talk to the Pastor about the problems at hand and I wouldn't just bust him out although I really wanted to. I thought then what type of wife would I have been to do that? I was literally crying on the inside. After the appointment it was like I could hear the devil laughing directly in my face. Really Tina... Did you think that little stunt would actually work? Now that I have him, I refuse to allow him to come back to you ever again, so you might as well just give up and throw in the towel. My heart was hurting so bad right now. I didn't know what to do next, then something rose up deep within me and said devil I refuse give up on my husband or our marriage and the fight from that day was on. Spiritual Warfare it is!!! This time I refuse to be defeated no matter what happens. Though it was difficult I had decided that if the Lord was with me then I know that I can trust him to be with me now. There were many things that I trusted Him for at that time because so much was going on but so little that I could do, I had to exercise faith yet again. This time how could I imagine things would turn out drastically different.

Just when I had begun to think that I had persuaded my husband that things were looking up for us, the road that we were traveling did a 360% turn in the other direction. I got the wind knocked out of me. One night we took a trip to Wal-Mart to get some things for the house and I had to pay a bill. I begged and pleaded with him to take me to the one located in West Bend just to spend some quality time with him. He said he was too busy to take that type of time out of his schedule so we went to the one up the street from our house. As I went inside he stayed behind to answer a call on his cell phone. I went inside alone. He came in for a brief moment and told me that he needed to meet someone outside. At the time I was upset because I knew what that meant. Now I understand why he wanted to go to that particular Wal-Mart. I looked up and saw a scuffle in the hallway and there were about six policemen chasing a man, then a fight, then they wrestled the man to the ground. As I looked a little closer the alleged man was none other than my husband. I ran out to the hallway to address the situation and they pushed me back inside the store and slammed the door. The police were handling my husband real rough so I started taping everything because I planned to press charges if he was hurt on any inch of his body. They opened the door then snatched my cell phone and erased everything that I had recorded. I began yelling and screaming because by this point, they were doing too much. Lord what in the world is going on. Later to find out my husband was meeting his cousin for a business transaction but he never came, but he sent the police instead. Not again I thought. This time wasn't sure how it would work out. I was so utterly afraid. He hadn't been out six months, on parole, third drug case, and our life was history.

There were so many thoughts flowing through my mind at this time. As these police were arresting my husband. What was I to do? I had spoken to my husband over and over again begging and pleading with him to stop doing what he was doing, to pray and trust God because things would be okay. He knew that I had been fighting my previous employer for a Workers Compensation claim and the attorneys were close to a settlement. Once that paid out our financial struggles would be okay. His statement to me was you pray, you trust God but I am going to do what needs to be done so that our family won't starve or end up on the streets. I asked repeatedly if I should quit school and get a job and that was not an option. He said you stay in school. You need your degree. He thought that we would be fine but in essence that was far from the truth. We were far from fine at this point. While we were at Wal-Mart, the police were at our door making every attempt to gain entry into our home. Our children were hesitant because they knew not to allow police inside without a search warrant. Finally the police told them a lie about a rapist being in the area and their need to check our house to make sure that everything was safe. Our daughter allowed them in. Now that they were in… my husband situation just turned from bad to worst. All of our children were home and our daughter had both of her children, our grandchildren. They finally allowed me to come out of the store only to tell me that my husband had just got caught in a major drug bust, he had been set up by a confidential informant, and was now facing time. They let me know that the police squad had entered our home and basically told me if I didn't provide permission (by signing a letter) they would take all our children and grandchildren and put them in foster care. I was so scared that I began to cry. Now I was about to lose everything, my husband, my children and my life. What was I to do? If I signed the letter I was going against my husband and if I didn't, I was not protecting my children and grandchildren. I looked at my husband and at that time, I chose our children. The look on his face could have killed me. Little did I know I didn't have to make either choice because if I had chosen to trust in God, he would have made everything work out despite of how it looked. I was put in one police car and my husband in another and we had no idea where we were being taken at that moment. I knew it was prison for at least one of us. We pulled up in front of our house shortly to see the police were there waiting. They had seized many items from our home which were enough to have my husband brought up on some serious charges. He could possibly be sent away for a long time. Before taking my husband off to prison they allowed us to talk briefly. The look on his face alone tore me up on the inside. I was furious and hurt and scared all at the same time. He looked at me and said, "Bay I am threw". I felt his pain because it not only affected him, it affected our entire family. Here we go again, I thought. With tears in my eyes I cried myself to sleep that night because my husband wasn't there and not sure when or if I would see him again anytime soon. I couldn't eat or sleep. I hadn't spoken to him for over a week. I honestly didn't know if he was dead or alive. I didn't answer anyone calls. I didn't answer my door. I didn't want to be bothered by anyone who couldn't fix this for me. I needed someone to tell me we would be alright and we could make it through this again. The only one who could wasn't answering me. Could he still hear my prayers or had we lost touch??? All I could think was I am not staying this time, I would get a divorce. I didn't ask to be here yet again and I didn't have to be. This is now his problem, not mine. I was fueled by my anger. Was I angrier at me for not being submissive or him for being so stupid? I had cried so much to where I couldn't cry any longer. The more I thought about this man and his decision to do what allowed him to be removed from our lives yet again not sure what I was about to do.

Today my phone rang and much to my surprise, it was a collect call from my husband who I hadn't spoken to for over a week. It was bitter sweet because he was sorry that he had put us through this situation again but he just couldn't see our family in such a horrible financial situation. He said baby I am so sorry for putting you in this situation and I now know that I can't serve two masters, I can't serve the devil and also serve God. He said God knew that I needed to be sat down in order to stop selling drugs!!! At that time a stream of tears ran down my face because I realized that my husband wasn't totally lost and the devil couldn't have his life. There was still hope for us, for our marriage and for our family. I was now faced with decisions to be made. He knew how I felt at that time and respected my choices whether it would be to stick by his side or to leave. He also reminded me of our marriage vows… for better or for worst and how we said *no divorce* before we were married. We had both agreed that this was it once we are married that divorce would never be an option. After we got off the phone that day I went into prayer for a few things because all I knew at that point was it would take God to keep me in the mist of this storm. I needed him now more than I ever had before because I didn't have a job or income, I wasn't receiving any public assistance and my husband was gone, yet again so was all of our money for the second time around. I needed to know what to do next. No friend could tell me, no family member, not my Pastor or 1st Lady, not even my mother or father only God could direct me. Listening to Him I knew that I was ordained to stay no matter what happened next.

It has been about 9 days now and my oldest son called me on my cell phone. I can't remember where I was at or what I was doing but he said Mom, you have something from your attorney that looks like a check. I said really!!! Open it and tell me what you see. There was a pause on the line for such a long time that I began to panic, something must be wrong, I thought but when he finally came back to the line, He said Mom there is a check in your name for $24,000. I couldn't breathe at that moment. I told my son I would be there shortly. All I could do was praise the Lord for delivering a ray of hope for our family. We now had some money to pay bills, to move forward and to live. After praying and thanking the Lord for increase, I consulted with my husband as to what we needed to do first, no Bail money this time because he would fight from inside; we needed to retain an attorney on his behalf. I set aside rent payments for next four months to get me through to tax time then paid as many bill collectors as possible to stay above water. I saved as much as possible to live off until I decided what to do next as far as employment. I had also gotten an unemployment extension so now I had income. The harder I worked at trusting God the more he open doors and provided for us. Through it all I missed my husband so such. I really wished I could wake up from this nightmare and things would go back to normal but what would represent normal for us? When he was home, we were barely talking, barely happy, barely doing things that normal married people are supposed to do. We both felt the same way, if we had took more time out to love one another through the trial this might be a little easier to bare. We couldn't even remember that last time that we were intimate and guess what it will be a long time before it will ever happen again but we were in a place where we had to have the desire to see this thing to the end whenever that might be. This time his case was hardcore because in four months of selling drugs, he had accumulated more than half of the money, drugs, and status that he had before he left the first time. He was facing a great deal of time. The attorney we had retained was one of the best criminal attorneys in the Milwaukee area who came highly recommended. He would do what he could but this ultimately would take a mighty move of God. The question was… Will we put our trust totally in Him?

It had felt like our life had been purposely placed at a standstill. We had been going back and forth to court with nothing happening and things didn't look good. With God being on our side it wasn't about what we saw but about what we believed. It was the most difficult thing but if God had done it before than what would be different now? There wasn't nothing that had changed because He was still God and stilled loved us despite of where we were in that present time in our lives. We had to stand on the promises of God. Tomorrow was court and I was sick all in my body because my husband life was on the line, and his freedom was at stake, so was mine because if he was locked up then how would I being his wife remain free. It didn't make any sense to me. I couldn't grab a hold of the entire situation. I didn't understand and it didn't make sense that day. He was sentenced to 13 years and 10 months that day. He would be gone for over 5 years without a doubt then come home with 8 years of strict adult supervision on parole. After that date we had many doubts as to whether we would make it through. We knew the road ahead would be rough but we also knew that with God for us then nobody could be against us. We faced some trying times with ups and downs on a regular basis but kept our faith. We prayed, trusted, and believed that no matter what it look like we would be reunited again stronger than we were the day that he had to leave.

I have faced many long days and cold nights since that day in October 2007 and my husband has been gone for over 5 years in the State of Wisconsin Prison System. There were many times when I could have given up but I chose not to, it was never by my own strength but by the strength of God. There have been many tests of our love, faithfulness, commitment, loyalty, strength, understanding and patience. Our love was tested because love is defined as an emotion of strong affection and attachment also the virtue of representing all of human kindness, compassion, and affection and the unselfish loyal and benevolent concern for the good of another. We both had to find others ways to show love in letters, visits and phone calls which at times was difficult but we found exciting ways to do just that. I had been tested many times in the area of faithfulness because there was always men coming around me and attempting to remind me of what I was missing which was the physical companionship of my husband. I missed the time we used to spend together whether it was going out to dinner, or watching a movie. I even missed a simple hug, holding hands, or a kiss. I was able to remain faithful, loyal and committed to my husband and our marriage covenant. By doing those things, it help to build a stronger bond between us. As the years went by our marriage became stronger in areas that might have otherwise been weak. It wasn't a bond built on intimacy but build by distance. We learned to understand one another and patiently wait for those things that we expected out of our marriage. My husband's relationship with God grew stronger and deeper and so did mine. We knew that it would take God in the center to see us through this storm. My Husband being incarcerated for us wasn't a situation of bondage for us but truly an experience of us being free. There is nothing more wonderful than being able to find the love of God in the midst of an unimaginable situation but being able to make it through together. Where we are today is just our beginning, the best is yet to come.

Apostle D Neal note: Mr. Mull, at publication of this book, is now home and they are building ministry and business together.

MEMOIRS OF SACRED
BY LATISHA PRICE

I found my true purpose through my failing marriage. It all started 10/10/2010 God exposed some truths about my husband in order to get my attention. Although these truths nearly took me out of here; through these trials I learned the true meaning of God's power. It took an affair, disrespect, strife, heartbreak and confusion for me to wake up and hear God calling me. His love for me and the love of my family broke the chains the devil tried to place on me. I want to tell a story that shows how God prevailed in my life. Not a story that depicts and degrades my husband's wrong doings or bad choices.

My husband had cheated plenty of times when we weren't married and to be honest I went into the marriage with the attitude "Oh well if it doesn't work at least I tried." With years and years of mental and emotional abuse, cheating and disrespect I still somehow found myself married to this man. Don't get me wrong my husband and I have an excellent friendship and to be honest we actually make better friends then we do a couple. But for some odd reason a force greater than I can understand keeps pulling us together even when it has been times we should have been far apart. Well to make a long story short I found out through this affair that our purpose together was greater than being married. Yes he is my husband but God has me in his life to help bring him back to His kingdom. See my husband was so far gone controlled by the enemy's tactics and spirits that it just appeared as though he was an empty vessel at times.

When I first met him in 1993 at the age of thirteen I had always felt like I was suppose to save him. I could see something in him that no one else could and I guess that's why I stayed continually all these years. Leading back up to that day I mentioned in the beginning of my story it was made clear to me that the man I married had other motives which were contrary to God's meaning of marriage. During that turn of event everything started out to be a blur and it felt as though my whole world crashed and burned. I spent several months in a state of warfare fighting to say my life. It felt like I was dying, I couldn't get out of the bed, go to work, eat, think or raise my son. This event took a toll on me because this time my husband had established a relationship with a young lady that was based off of more than just sex. This feeling he developed with this girl changed the whole dynamics of our marriage and took a large piece of my existence. A piece of me that left me numb to the world but opened up my heart and ears to hear God speak.

Apostle D. Neal note: there is nothing too hard for God. When we come out from our hiding places, we see HIM, and what He's doing in our marriages.

IT'S NEVER THE END

Every lesson in life should be shared with others; it should be shared no matter what the end result is, because it is a testimony that God is able and ever present. Each marriage represented here, is a testimony of how God keeps you; how, even though, there are ups and downs, He gives us an answer: wait.

Even if its only prayer, you have God by your side. Even if you have a great marriage, you have a testimony of God's grace, favor and mercy. Let me remind you that you are not alone! We are here for you! I am here to guide you, but God will lead you. It is never the end.

Let me also add, that even if you are at the crossroads of staying in the marriage or going for divorce, I'm separated right now, but the divorce hasn't been finalized. God can change ANYTHING. I trust HIM that the place my husband and I are in right now today (5/16/2014) is where we need to be.

It is never the end! God bless you!

Apostle D. Neal

www.ingramcontent.com/pod-product-compliance
Lightning Source LLC
Chambersburg PA
CBHW071022040426

42443CB00007B/907